Invisible Woman

Other books of poetry by JOYCE CAROL OATES

Anonymous Sins and Other Poems (1969)
Love and Its Derangements (1970)
Angel Fire (1973)
The Fabulous Beasts (1975)
Women Whose Lives Are Food,
    Men Whose Lives Are Money (1978)

Ontario Review Press Poetry Series

INVISIBLE WOMAN

New & Selected Poems 1970–1982
by
JOYCE CAROL OATES

ONTARIO REVIEW PRESS
Princeton, New Jersey

Many of the new poems in this collection were first published, in different versions, in *The Atlantic Monthly* ("The Present Tense," "The Wasp"), *The Georgia Review* ("First Death, 1950," "Back Country"), *Harper's* ("Baby"), *The Hudson Review* ("Night Driving, New Year's Eve," under the title "Night Driving, New Year's Eve 1976"; "Leavetaking, at Dusk," under the title "Leavetaking"; "The Proofs of God"; "Another"), *The Iowa Review* ("F____"), *The Kenyon Review* ("The Child-Bride"), *Mademoiselle* ("There Are Northern Lakes. . . ."), *The Malahat Review* ("The Stone Orchard"), *The Missouri Review* ("Query, Not To Be Answered," under the title "Query"), *The Nation* ("Footprints"), *The New Republic* ("Jesus, Heal Me"), *The Ontario Review* ("Ecstasy of Flight," "Ecstasy of Motion," "Ecstasy of Boredom at the Berlin Wall"), *The Paris Review* ("A Report to an Academy," "First Dark"), *The Southern Review* ("Nightless Nights," "High-Wire Artist"), *The Texas Quarterly* ("Psalm," "Appetite and Terror on the Wide White Sands of Western Florida," under the title "Appetite. Terror."), *The Virginia Quarterly Review* ("The Loss," "Boredom," "Last Things").

Broadsides of "Snowfall" (1978) and "The Stone Orchard" (1980) were published by the Lord John Press.

Some of these poems appeared in limited editions published by Black Sparrow Press (*Season of Peril*, 1977), William B. Ewert (*Nightless Nights*, 1981), and Pressworks (*Celestial Timepiece*, 1981).

Poems selected from *Angel Fire, The Fabulous Beasts,* and *Women Whose Lives Are Food, Men Whose Lives Are Money* reprinted by permission of Louisiana State University Press.

Library of Congress Cataloging in Publication Data

Oates, Joyce Carol, 1938-
   Invisible woman.

   (Ontario Review Press poetry series)
   I. Title.   II. Series.
   PS 3565. A815   811'.54   81-22402
                         AACR2
   ISBN 0-86538-015-5
   ISBN 0-86538-016-3 (pbk.)
   ISBN 0-86538-021-X (deluxe)

Distributed by PERSEA BOOKS, Inc.
225 Lafayette St.
New York, NY 10012

For my husband, Raymond

The danger in happiness. Now everything I touch turns out to be wonderful: Now I love any fate that comes along. Who would like to be my fate?

—Nietzsche

CONTENTS

I.

Sun-Truths

Invisible Woman

What are the legends we invent,
  what are the tales spun of us
  in rooms we leave too quickly—

What is our transparency but the fact
  of flesh, the angry ache in the loins,
  that old betrayal—

"A face is a poor guarantee," says Montaigne,
  but bodies must be entered.
Because you know me, we have never met.
Because you see me, you cannot hear.

The Stone Orchard

Slowly, by day, in the cold sun of autumn,
the pears harden to green. To stone.

They are shrinking to stone,
to peevish greeny peace.

This is the logic of hatred:
they cannot ripen, or fall.

This is the logic of chastity:
the facial mask too tight to age.

Slowly, by day, with the sun as a witness,
the pears of the orchard turn to stone.
The trees ache. The old limbs sag.
Their discomfort is too curious to be tragic.

Who has warned us against this hard bitter taste?—
the small flat dead pleasure of stony fruit.
I love it, the bitterness,
the peevish chill.
The chastity of stone.

I stride through the stone orchard
immense with satisfaction.
I own this, and *I own this.*
The stony weight, the pitiless density.
The logic of hatred.

Nightless Nights

Midsummer.
The North.
And the eye never closes.

The giant's eye.
Unsleeping.
The great brain. Dreaming.

And you in the dream.
You no longer you.
In the great pale yolk of an eye.
In the brain's machinery.
Unceasing.

Midnight.
And dawn.
All creation heaved together.
Racing pulse, beating wings,
a twilight of creatures' cries—

And you in the machinery,
you no longer you.

A moon that is a sun burns over your left shoulder.
The pulsebeat in your eye is a frenzy.
Morning!—and night!—
and you mute at the center!

Sightless gaze, no words,
your body's tide rising helpless with the light.
It is eternal light.
It is a perfect clockwork.

The great eye transfixes you,
all creation is heaved together,

can you resist?
Wordless.

Midsummer.
The North.
The Night.

The Wasp

O the instrument draws close,
very close.
The wasp is silent.

Gowned and gloved and regal
the surgeon makes his perfect
incision, O watch.

Don't flinch: a deep inky hair
from the base of the skull to the parietal.
It cannot hurt, such thin trickling blood!

O the rubber fingers peel back the scalp,
the sticky scalp. Lie still.
When the bone is exposed the air hums.

O the wasp is now in a fury,
a sudden fury.
His crevice, *his* cavity—so close!

Maddened buzzing and flailing papery wings,
O the tiny holes are drilled with *such*
precision!

And the membrane is cut,
and the bone swung out,
and the air tickles,
and the wasp is cunning-silent.

O the instrument draws close,
very close:
a three-inch silver tweezers.

O graceless as lead you lie still,
and grateful.

The wasp is removed: a tiny fury.
It buzzes in its rage, O don't flinch!—

though the tweezers has pinched it in two.

Heavily you sleep, saved,
and too feeble to protest.
Why do we think we must live forever?
The instrument rudely wipes
the wasp on a cotton pad.
O don't flinch!—it is over.
You are grateful.

Last Things

Combing my hair, a sudden snarl
in the pink plastic teeth.

How silent, death entering.

But I mean of course only the thought.
The thought of death.
The thought of Death.

I mean of course only the thought,
entering.

Season of Peril

It is the Season of Peril,
the time of quick growth.
The grasses cry aloud in their labor.
Tent-caterpillars drop one by one,
    writhing pellets of flame.
The jays shriek, thick black lengths of snake
are thawing, the first eyelid trembles,
the first eye opens.

And who is this, they murmur in packs.
Who dares such miracles?—
the God-Child tottering on stilts,
in contempt of the earth.
Small and mean and quick, their hands slapping at him.

    Tunnel and nudge, burrow with your head,
pry, beg, love, wound,
into the deepest region of the body.
Where no soul resides. And no memory.
There, there is carbon.
Carbon, and water, and salt.
But no voice, and no peril.

Baby

Four walls, a ceiling, and the baby grows.
Floorboards, blinded windows. Airless air.
And the baby grows.

Weeks and hours,
clambering toward you:
a plump wattled purse.

The baby grows enormous with the calendar.
Cherub-fat, quivering thighs and buttocks,
snorts of laughter escape you at the sight.
Wet wide lips, a carnivore smile, *Love me.*

Bare floor, a windowsill edged with grime.
Years have passed. *Love and feed.* The baby grows
mollusc-smug, enormous. Cannot now be stopped.
Lurid flushed cheeks, jewels for eyes.
Ah, a Cupid-toad! And yours.
Inside these walls, below this ceiling,
yours. Cannot be stopped.

Love and feed. Swollen sausages for fingers.
He grows filling the room, the space. You.
Fat knees cutely dimpled. Ears pink and delicate
as shells. O Love you are enormous, clambering
toward me, filling the room, the space.
The air glistens. There is no air.
The baby grows.

A Miniature Passion

All I want, I boldly said,
is to keep you from dying, with my love:
and the wasp's sting was so deep,
all my flesh was a crater to it.

Sun-Truths

The artery beat hard in your throat, they said,
just beneath the jaw.
What is its name?
I like to think I might have stroked it calm.

Your face was a ravaged orange moon, they said,
in fact it wasn't yours at the end.
I don't believe them.

Was there an autopsy?
I can't ask.

You told me: Any dwarf of a god, we might try to befriend!—
but what of idiot chance?

All the clocks beat, solemn and assured
they will beat forever.

     In your grandmother's high old house
you seized my wrist, you said, Look!—
the clock's pendulum has stopped,
now we can read the engraving!—
but the gold pendulum was smooth,
and not gold.

The proposition is: Flesh has memory.
The proposition is: Flesh has memory
but is perpetually innocent.
Even in ripening, even in rot.

I am not angry at your death,
I don't see myself shouting into your face.

The problem is: Invisible now,

you are everywhere.

     You said: I can't bear sun-truths,
they're too harsh. I prefer the moon—
that gauze, that sickly echo, that "wisdom."

The Mourning

A fist of cold striking your face.
Each smiling crease made permanent.
I am not I, so bereft.
I have always been young.

Tears solid as pebbles,
trivial as pebbles, tears and words.
Again, the words. The same tears.
Again and still again,
the same
words, the tears,
the mourning,
the cold,
the same.

The Mourning II

Your death is the great white hulk of a monument
we continue to circle, groping
for the featureless face,
guessing at the positions of hands, arms, legs,
puzzling over the way inside.

The Loss

The loss you can't remember.
A thumb-smeared wall, the mind's stupor.
The haze at the horizon, the loss
indistinct, the stammered words
repeating themselves.
You can't remember.

"A strange oblivion has overspread me,"
Samuel Johnson wrote.
His sky lowered itself into a squat.

      The loss that is a coin, tossed
boldly in air, then falling from the palm
to clatter away—a gutter, a drain—
the loss you have already forgotten,
the loss no more than a taste in the mouth.

I suppose you thought, cunning and slippery as an eel,
you would always be the thief—
and never the victim?

The loss in the mirror, the invisible
face, the loss you discover too late,
pawing at your pocket: but where?
The great sky itself in a squat,
overspreading.
Tears and words that repeat,
repeat.
But what?—
You can't remember.

Poem Jubilant in Place of Mourning

Wedding day all day, and the cake twelve white tiers high,
and everyone has been photographed, and the tulips have opened,
the Sand-Man is thumping his heels on the stairs, the Sand-Man
is a tiresome old legend, isn't the wedding cake delicious?—
And the bride amidst her presents, grinning into a plastic cup.

The entire world, root to cloud, was encased in fluffy white
frosting, the kind you lick off the big stirring spoon, the kind
that sticks in your eyelashes, yet I heard the Sand-Man
on the stairs, the Sand-Man poking and prying at the wedding
presents, an old dirge, an old limerick, we stared at each other,
we shook hands, Haven't we met before?—atop the twelve-
tiered wedding cake!

My fingers caressed your face, it didn't dismay me that
the eyes were gone, we know the principle of inner wisdom,
we know the principle of spiritual strength, and what of
stoicism, consider the red-streaked tulips, consider the bridal veil,
wedding day all day, from root to cloud, the string quartet has
begun, an interested observer asked you *Now that the Sand-Man has
plucked out your eyes, please give us your opinion
of the global situation*, and you replied *The trouble with "eternal
moments" is that there are too many of them*—

(Reverent silence,
a scattering of embarrassed applause,
the Sand-Man uncorking a bottle
of noisy champagne.)

Wedding day all day, Easter Sunday soon, lilies and chocolate eggs,
and then Christmas, the bridegroom wiping saliva from the bride's
red lips, Fourth of July and cannon, frankfurters, confetti of
New Year's Eve, followed swiftly by Hallowe'en and Ash Wednesday
and Lincoln's Birthday, now that your eyes are gone are we all
invisible to you, are we all the same din?—the Sand-Man striking
a beefy fist against the bedroom door, you would smile at his
polka-dot bowtie, you would be patient with the father of the bride,

that sad drunk, a pity you can't melt this sugar rosebud on your tongue,
a pity you can't hear this old quartet by Borodin that always
lacerates the heart.
It always does.

II.

The Forbidden

The Forbidden

The relief not to be uttered,
the syllables not mouthed.
The mirrored door that flies open so swiftly
you see yourself in flight.
How alive, how alive,
how unexpected.

Honeymoon

My face in the frame of your fingers.
Bedsheets writhing like snakes.

Drowning in sweat. The great angry fist of your heart
beating against my ribs.

In sleep you blunder
against me, murmuring.
Old hurts, old wrongs, a prayer that has the taste
of blood.
Fingers gripping my mouth.
My foot hard on your shoulder.

A fleck of blood in your eye.
Toes, twenty, twitching!—and all so lively.
Blue noon lazily pulsing against the walls
where years have passed.
The chain on the door has rusted. The lock.
The machine runs on, fed shuddering
with quarters.

Someone's heart at a gallop now,
a brain trapped in nightmares.
It is all very casual.
It is all very domestic.

My pulse leaps in your throat,
a strand of your hair catches
between my grinning teeth.
Years have passed in the hollows of these bedsheets.
So close, we are invisible to each other.
And no one can see us.

There Are Northern Lakes. . . .

There are northern lakes where fish swim engorged
with cold in the blaze of August.
Where your body, solid meat, would freeze
if it plunged into that featureless sky.

There are cysts the size of a needle's blind eye
that swell with the spring like an old love
tickling your quiet to a frenzy.
There is a ray of pain secret,
in the scissors' double point.

And the creature that swims ungainly
through the inky seaweed. . . .
It rises to brush its lips against yours,
it sinks back again, into an abyss of dozing eyes.
It is immense, it is blind, it is skeletal, it is jelly.
Innocent as a bridal veil.

The sinew that connects you is slender as a shadow.

Tachycardiac Seizure

You rebound from one wall to another,
running, no windows, no door, smooth white walls
shaking with a rhythmic tremor, it is terror,
it is terror become boredom, hypnotic as windshield
wipers, the calm of panic past strength, you are run-
ning, you dare not stop, the heartbeat is too urgent,
you must not listen, you must not take your pulse,
what if your heart explodes, only wait, have patience,
you cannot die inside such familiar walls
and if you do—

    —They will open the bolted door,
they will hoist you above the pounding floorboards,
they will carry you away bodiless
as an old legend.

The Proofs of God

Children are clamoring for the proofs of God.
Beneath their pillows?—round blank buttons.
Their silky baby locks, outgrown, lie in drawers
amid twine and thumbtacks and old report cards
and packets of seeds never opened.

There are competing theologies:
you must never eat animal fiber,
you must never inhale plastic,
you dare not contemplate the lunar eclipse
save through an isosceles triangle.
Never doubt with your full strength, the Church Fathers say.

They have been *there*, after all.
And have returned.
Unfortunately they remember very little.

Ah, here, a packet of sepia photographs,
or are they only old postcards
scrawled over in an unfamiliar hand . . . ?
And unreadable.

The proofs of God fly into our faces out of old leatherbound books,
shaken loose from old attic clothes,
old maps of North America.
Old now themselves, the children still clamor.
What are the proofs of God, they insist.

    Miniature proofs will suffice,
    small enough to be carried in a spoon.

Another

Another dusk: coldly whitely blue,
and the great spruces humbled with snow,
again the western distance bruised with sun,
again the stillness seeping
out of the earth's core.

Another dusk, and it is that moment
when the heart falters at such beauty—
though isn't it routine,
smug as clockwork?
Why must you interpret everything as a sign?
As if you wanted to be injured!

Another dusk: deepening now into night,
and again the reflection in the window
floating in the mock depth of the glass,
taking ghost-colors out of the night.

Yes—another dusk, and why
must you stare melancholy and smiling?—
as if everything were new,
as if night had no history,
and that woman's face in the window,
so suddenly visible, a baptism
into a prodigious self.

Another dusk: deepening into night.

Leavetaking, at Dusk

The house is empty, nearly.
It thinks nothing now, it has given away its secrets
cheaply.

Room after room,
the blankness of walls
we have not seen before.
Bare hardwood floors. Geometrical precision.
Dusk flattened like a stranger's face
against the north windows.

The house is no one's now,
it is nothing human.
A past and a future, but no present.

We pass through it, invisible.
Now the ceilings rise.
A lone mad cricket sings in a corner.

Night Driving, New Year's Eve

Plunging west into the snowy dusk of New York State,
there is no end to it: snakes that writhe in the headlights,
twisting scarves of snow, veins and vines and tendrils,
the sky broken in pieces
hard as crockery.

Flying above the shredded clouds,
thousands of feet above the ground.
Weightless, bodiless, borne along by the wind
foam-heavy waves leap and break
and turn to mist, to eels,
snapping back upon themselves.

Night driving, hour upon hour. Eyes unresisting.
A pleased dumb hurt floods the brain.
Am I exhausted, am I in danger?—
the highway is a rushing river,
figures at the roadside beckon,
trees and swans and children and pillars and stairways,
moons, gorgons, God.
And the dead with their patient faces,
who do not appear to be dangerous.

Am I still on the earth's surface, or soaring above?—
I see below a cloud of white mayflies.

Sinews of snow, pellets of snow,
impish as children: and lovely.
There is no end to it.
Hour upon hour drunken eels fly past the windshield,
the Void is as familiar as a billboard,
the spectres by the roadside are old companions.
A northern wind lifts a corner of the universe
and the car rushes forward into that space,
my hands firm on the wheel.

The road passes beneath,
memory passes beneath,
it is a snowy dusk in New York State,
it is the famous New Year,
somewhere up ahead.

Betrayal

The hollow voice,
the megaphone words.
The eyes with their slits
for pupils. Blind?

I do not know you, the voice intones.
We have never met, the plaster head nods.
We have not been lovers, brag the lips.

You are wiped off with a forefinger
thick as a cigar.

Good Morning

You can't swallow the stone shoved into your mouth.
It lies heavy on the tongue, and about it
saliva bubbles: your serious need is *not to drown.*
And you dare not move because of the wires
threaded through your eyes.
And the mud.
Tarry. Slick. Hoof-sized.
In the pit of the gut.

And none of this can be transposed.

Suddenly you wonder what the language is for—
except *Good morning! how are you! isn't it a fine morning!*
Except to shout *Happy Birthday! Congratulations on the baby!*
Looks as if it will clear by noon!
And you're looking fine too.

A burdock lodged between your ribs, an angry wasp
in your skull, minnows coursing through your veins,
and the stone, the great stone, the prodigious stone
in your mouth: not to be transposed.

It *is* a good morning.
It *will* clear by noon.
But the mud is still here, and you are still here.
Tarry, hoof-sized.
In the pit of the gut.

Query, Not To Be Answered

For instance, why
does the blood coagulate:
why does the tiny mouth of a wound
turn prim when touched by air:
why don't we drain away
like fluid in cracked vases?

Why are there certain weathers
that contract giants to shadows:
that reduce the splendor of our voices
to echoes: the bloom of our souls
to mere seeds?

And why is it that the dead
move so airily among us,
claiming so little,
claiming us?
In their presence even answers become queries.

Appetite and Terror on the
Wide White Sands of Western Florida

Wind and sun and sky and appetite sucking and smacking like the ocean.
Then again terror. Simple, complete.

Look again, it is wonderfully hungry, it is zestfully greedy,
in fact it is only a stomach with a brain.

But now it hesitates, it convulses with a thought,
has something frightened it?

When it is picturesque one should take pictures.
A dozen sandpipers on delicate legs
flowing like sunshine across the debris: so graceful.
Now it is a terrier nuzzling a spine, scales, fins.
Now it is a child in inexplicable white satin, shivering,
     on the wide stucco steps of the Seacrest Inn.

The pelicans drooping like old men waiting crankily to die,
the seagulls shrieking in fright,
or in ecstasy. Much flapping of wings. Beaks, scaly feet. Claws.
A woman in a white mink stole, her high heels sinking in sand,
a pretty clumsiness, bracelets clattering,
now it scuttles across the tough-ribbed beach
as the northeast wind whips your hair,
now it flies up on massive panicked wings.

A giant conch comes clattering at your feet.

Appetite, the waves crest and foam and suck, terror, a dog
is yipping, the jellyfish can sting, the jellyfish are all water,
here is the remains of a wondrous fish with a jewel for an eye,
here is a magnificent cobweb with a jewel trembling at its center,
appetite and terror, now appetite, now the stomach and jaws,
the greed, the terror, the scuttling of legs, the wild fluttering
of wings, *Trissie!* cries the woman cupping her hands to her mouth

Trissie come here! she cries,
but neither the terrier nor the child responds,
even the sandpipers race past unhearing.

Psalm

Suppose you had been lovers once, you and this dying man.
Suppose you had raised that flush to his face, once.
The amazing glow of blood. The real thing.
About which there are ancient psalms, and jokes.
But the real thing, once.

Suppose you are a witness now to the flow
stinging into that large meek vein.
Suppose as you watch the vein turns black, turns
hard, a many-branched tree: a kind of prehensile skeleton.

Suppose you think: The Allegory of the Cave will save us.
Or that old psalm of *valleys*, *shadows*, *death*.
There is a balance in all things, there is wit in his grimace,
and, as always, the telephone directory to guide you—
how *Aa* proceeds to *Zy*. How the living damp heart
of the great forest proceeds to pulp, to be crumpled
in any hand.

Snowfall

Snowfall upon the ice-locked river snowfall
across the glittering valley snow falling onto my palm
the patient turning of snow falling this evening
last Sunday the snowfall of next January crystallizing
in massive cloud canyons

Snowfall we whisper like beads snow we have memorized
and named with the names of saints the snow falling
upon your warm tongue bristling angry as bees against
the window the snowfall that is coughing, that is the mad
white eyes of geese, the snowfall of sand and of calcium,
the falling of snow soft as a moth's down, snowfall like
a lover's eyelashes brushing your cheek, like your cry
muffled in the snow falling in the pine forest, the invisible
weight crushing your skull out of shape, snowfall gentle
as a kiss, murmurous as the sea in your ears, like sleep,
like blindness, like tiny halting stitches in the flesh,
silent as a moonblind night

Snow-Drunk in Ontario

Midday the sudden ferocity of sleet!—
midnight in April and the house rocks, rocks,
a great weary heart bucking the waves.

And this morning—ah, this morning!—
a whirlwind of sun clattering gay
as a pinwheel.

Too much light and we can't see,
too much April light and we are blinded,
two drunks clutching hands,
one marriage, one life,
filling up with snow.

Snow has drifted to the foot of the bed,
ice packs us hard beneath the sheets,
snug as tulip bulbs, gaily
immortal.

The earth's axis, it seems, has shifted.
According to authorities no one is to blame.

Palm Sunday in April and we are snow-drunk,
jaunty sailors bucking the great ocean's waves.
In our youth we made ridiculous claims.
We will live arrow-swift
drawn back and released from the tightest of bows!—
Or, *We will live simply, sunflowers nodding,*
fish in muck, cumulous clouds.

Now all is changed. Now the wild snow flies.
In April, in Ontario, clutching hands,
drunk at the prow of the old heaving ship.
A ragged flag whips above.
The sun clatters gay as a pinwheel.
We are, we suppose, supremely happy,
and what of that?—
hail bounces down our roof.

Footprints

A clownish stumbling in the snow last night,
footprints bold outside our windows,
circling the house as we slept. . . .

Who wanted entry into our lives, who pressed
against our darkened windows,
who stood invisible at the edge of our dreaming . . . ?

III.

First Dark

First Dark

First dark. The exuberance of the night.
Insects in their music.
Razor-ribbons of noise.

First dark, and green wet air,
close as a breath.
My feet are damp, my fingers snatch at weed-flowers
drowsy with pollen, it is long ago,
I am not yet born, I am invisible,
prowling forbidden in first dark,
far from the lighted house.

At the pond the young frogs leap with their new legs,
small yelps of green. Sheer emerald.
You can't imagine. You can't exaggerate
that green.
Or the surprise, the yelps and leaps,
the splashes in the water,
small emeralds of alarm.
The way they disappear one by one
as you approach.

I am prowling, my feet are damp.
I am snatching at things to prove my life.
Wait!—where are you going!
That child I have never seen except in snapshots,
and cannot love,
where are you going?—isn't this forbidden?

How small the soul, cupped in a child's hand.
Held over the pocked water.
Ready to leap, and sink, and disappear.

Autistic Child, No Longer Child

Flywheel, whirligig, hummingbird, singing the same
cruel tune, a drone, a dirge, a nursery tune, which year
have we now, which birthday?—kitchen-bright the eyes,
rubber-smooth the skin,
your gaze slyly hooded,
your grin fierce in place.

So quick!—so cute!—monkey-nimble in your mock dance,
which season is this now, which anniversary, inside
the rocking waste motion, left to right to left,
the silence you wetly chew like your lips, the lullaby,
the hum, left to right, which year?—inside your empty stare,
what voltage?

        I cannot look into you
as into a mirror, though you mirror me, sister,
and were born on my birthday eighteen years after me
and late, very late.

Now you crackle with spirit, on Sundays most dead,
now you navigate the room, left to right, the relentless tune,
the moon-blank stare, what year have we now, what weather?—
how far it carries, your cheerful baby-dirge!

You hear us but will not, O never!
You see us but cannot, O no one dares force you,
what an insult to your soul!

To touch you, sister, is to feel that voltage.

To touch you, sister, is not our privilege.

Jesus, Heal Me

At the kitchen table life is opened
impatiently as a newspaper.
It is a strategy others seem to have mapped.
It is a crossword puzzle others seem to have solved.

Jesus touches your shoulder lightly,
lightly—not wanting to alarm.

Someone has strode angrily into the back yard,
smoking his cigar.
Coughing, hacking, Jesus the meek,
Jesus the impatient,
Jesus red-faced with rage.

Lay-offs, the union, the last meeting
when too many arrived,
always too many,
and not enough folding chairs
and no coffee.
Jesus the brother,
eyes like glaring coins.

The time-clock, the punch-card, the wrinkled paper
bag brought home again, to be used again.
The asphalt parking lot with all the puddles.
The plant the owners dare not close.
Time-and-a-half, and an ale after work,
the same faces in the tavern, the same
bottles, and at home someone is shouting,
or is it next door, a drunk shouting at a dog. . . .

Here, in the kitchen, someone yawns loudly.
Toes splayed, an old accident.
Don't remember. Jesus heals.
The newspaper is opened to columns of lottery winners.
The chair creaks in sudden hope.

Back Country

From the field behind our house, a low howling.
Slow drawn-out bleats of pain.
It was his boy's dog, therefore his, so he had every right
to grab the .22, and shoot:
his blood-threaded eyes are glazed with piety.

The dog was always hungry, he says.
The dog was in the way, the dog was vicious,
her tail was always slapping his legs.

Now his three children run to us, to hide,
even the fifteen-year-old is crying,
wanting the cellar. And not for the first time.

An August afternoon, very slow.
The first shot missed the heart, flew through the belly,
the second shot evidently went wild,
by the third Nellie had fled into the road,
yipping pain in ribbons, bright red confetti,
we had never heard anything like it before.

Our neighbor was too drunk to give chase.
There was no sport to it: he fired again, into the air.
Nellie dragged herself into our yard
where she snapped at my brother.
Howling on three legs she ran to our back field.
And now she is out there, dying.
But it is a noisy procedure.
It is not so easy as one might think.

In the meadow, in sweet clover,
O finally. Finally. An hour and ten minutes by the clock.
We can't call the police, my mother says, we can't make
trouble my grandmother says, they are thinking of our neighbor's wife,
they are thinking of the children, and of the gun.

Across the slouching wire fence he shouted words
we could not hear. Not sober but apologetic.
A little frightened. The rifle, the noise, the upset,
the trespass into another's yard.

My father comes home from work and my mother tells him
and he says very little, he goes out to bury the dog,
he doesn't want us with him, and then he goes next door to talk,
it is not for the first time, he talks, our fathers talk,
not for the first time, and then he returns,
his face leaden with disgust,
his skin flushed and mottled.
But he says nothing to us.

These things happen,
dogs get in the way.

First Death, 1950

in memory of my grandfather John Bush

With each, dies a piece of the old
life, which he carries. . . .
—William Carlos Williams

You crossed the Atlantic to quarrel in Hungarian, and drink,
and collapse, and die over an autumn weekend,
in astonishment gone mute for once:
and how the family wept,
in wise terror of the Angel of Death!

It was his time, they said.

You crossed the heaving ocean with no pity for your own flesh,
unmindful of the flame-rimmed smokestacks of the New World,
that gave no heat, but paid a surprising wage.
And you had no time to observe the storm of steel fragments
about your head like gnats, or your eyes socketed with grime,
or your face and hands and forearms encrusted with filth
that could never be wholly scrubbed away.
It was his time, they said.

False to say now that I loved you,
or that I even knew you.
Or could guess how your tender lungs bled, in secret,
how the steel filings burrowed like worms,
like larvae, hatching in your blood.
How your misshapen fingers never meant to hurt
twisting in play in my curls.

It was his time, they said.

Helpless in prayer, in ignorance,
rosaries clattering in ignorance,
but didn't the doctor too say *It was his time*,
weren't the hospital records succinct,
and the monthly pension came through, thank God,
and the A.F. of L. insurance,
and the coarse gray soap you used was thrown away,

and your filth-stiffened clothes,
and the jaunty "railroad" cap,
and there were no more drunken shouts on Friday night,
no more barks of laughter,
jokes and quarrels and flights of whimsy in Hungarian,
no more nights disturbed by your angry hacking cough.

It was your time to die, everyone agreed,
and I dare not record how young you were,
or why no one was to blame,
no one at fault, the rosaries, the prayer books,
the hospital you had never seen before,
the final brisk scrubbing.

For whose fault is the Angel of Death?—
sifting downward like newsprint
like blackened snow, perpetual
in Buffalo's wide winter:
Buffalo   Lackawana   Tonawanda

named for other blameless deaths.

Celestial Timepiece

By squares, by inches, hour upon hour
the great quilts grew.
Serendipity and *Felicity* and *All-Hallows-Eve*
and *Wonder-Working Providence* and *Milky Way*
and *Celestial Timepiece*—plants, suns, fireballs, moons—
covering half a wall
like a conqueror's map.

The men, the husbands, drew up such maps.
Their strategy has always been maps.

Look at these massive wool-and-feather-lined quilts,
recording square by square these wondrous years—
1784, 1806, 1848—
Glass Garden survives though frayed, and *Fools* and *Poppies*,
and *Gyroscope* all aflame, of 1864.

Soldiers are always passing along the roads.
Soldiers, the dead, prisoners in churches.
A hospital in a churchyard, the women's fingers working,
1865, 1876, conquerors on horseback along the roads,
Butterflies and *Christmas Eve* and *Jesus Our Savior*.

Square by square, spilling to the floor.
Winter days when the sun was a brief parenthesis overhead.
Spring days when no letters came. No news.
Calla lilies for the dead, gowns for the infants,
sunflowers bawdy as the first day of Creation.
Years. Decades. Centuries. Rags
torn from sheets, torn from dresses and trousers,
here is the resurrection of the body!—in the quilt's soiled squares.

The men's maps too are tearing,
so often folded.
The soldiers, the dead.
The conquerors on horseback.

She takes your hand, *Feel this, feel each square*, she says,
do you understand?
So many textures, a Babel of textures—coarse wool, fine silk,
satin, lace, burlap, cotton, brocade, hemp, fussy pleats—
you close your eyes, *Can you read it?* she asks, *Do you understand?*

Here, an entire world stitched to perfection.
By squares, by inches. You are the child-witness.
Your fingers read it like Braille.

for Robert Phillips

If you stare long enough it becomes beautiful.
O look: if you translate its *colors* into comely *sounds:*
ochre, russet, coppery-pink, nutmeg.
Soon it is an anti-world,
another way of seeing.

An industrial slum gaily glaring in a midsummer squall.
Your car slows, you are hypnotized, the sickly air has trapped you.
How porous smoke rises heavy and leaden-pale as a giant's thigh,
how the air heaves visibly in gusts,
sulphurous peonies blooming in the wind.
Here, an ancient sea-bed
guarded by a fifteen-foot Hercules fence.
Clouds break companionably about the highest smokestacks.
There is no amazement to the factory windows, opaque with grime,
as they slant open into the 100° shade.

What is there to say about these regions of our earth,
these domestic hells, these landscapes familiar
as high-tension wires whining overhead,
throbbing power on all sides?
Scars' stitchings in the earth. Miracle rainbows in the air.
What is there to say, why the wish to interpret,
to make judgments,
to record a vision?

If you stare long enough it translates into language.
The base of the pyramid—of course.
The history of labor in North America, the billyclubs, the militia,
the Pinkerton's men, the slaughter, the bleeding eyes, the barbed wire.
This is the base of the pyramid as always but it is not strewn with
                                                        workers' bones.
It glowers and winks instead with their acres of parked cars.

O acres, acres!—acres of parked cars. And all American,
and all very new.

Is the air noxious?—but you are the one who has weakened.

You are the one who ponders, which creatures graze in these pastures,
which monsters brood beside such rancid ponds—
mutant fish, giant crab-spiders of wire and rust,
toads with swollen white bellies,
armored things with spiny tails and eyes that stare unmoved
from the tops of stalks.

You are the sole observer to see *Ford* wittily obscured by grime,
to *F*— .
You are the only eye to record a plastic wreath at the top
of the highest smokestack, which you have been seeing for months:
Joy to the World   Gilmore Chemicals

Or is it another anti-world,
another way of seeing?

The Present Tense

in which I live hurtles airless a razor's swift slash
so deep there is no blood for the first instant no pain
except to the brain's eye the present tense is crammed
with fictitious memories curling snapshots in albums
the cheerful pretense of a history shared as we share stanzas
of coy old love songs no one ever sings

the present tense in which I live is a morning of Canada geese
passing overhead in their uncanny formations crying to one another
in a language I can't decode and the single deer bounding
through our woods graceful as if this were the Morning of Creation
the present tense is a telephone ringing and a stranger's raw voice
Who is that? and my own *Who is that?*—the Sand-Man on his way,
a husband I never married—and then the dial tone the seamless
present tense

it might be called a rosary as the moments slip by smooth
as beads worn by ancient fingers smooth as flimsy prayers
that rise to the lips in numbed panic or in comfortable routine
though just as reasonably it is the frantic buzz of a wasp trapped
between windows or in the skull or yawning in the daffodil-bright
sunshine or whispering psalms in honor of the dead

it is embraces and Valentine kisses and a soul small enough
to be carried in a spoon it is gaily aswarm with flying seeds
in celebration of those sequoias that live forever but are only
legends in this part of the world it might be that drawer
of snarled string and loose nails and the cats' matted hairbrush
it makes the charge *Now the day is passing, now the day is gone,*
what did the day mean, why did you see so little—

the present tense in which I live hurtles airless you forget
you haven't breathed for minutes a Chopin cadenza too swift
to be heard the birds startling up from the ledge in an explosion
of sleek grackle wings the present tense flies overhead too swift

to be grammatical it is all one stammered syllable shared
as we share songs we never sing it is all we know
it might be heaven, or hell,
or all we know

IV.

A Report to an Academy

Ecstasy of Flight

You are not you
at such a height.
Strapped in the fiery air.

You are not you
at such speed.
Such weapons.

Below, "nations" and "history"
pass silently.
Miniature worlds,
invisible spires.
Absurd fluttering flags.

The plane's swift shadow is benign—
but swift.

The next hour, the next season,
fiery air all around,
a routine miracle.
You are not you
in your pressurized container.

It has already happened.
Weapons, but not revenge.
Revenge is not in our interest.

Soon, your prayer is soon,
it has already happened,
perhaps it will happen soon,
perhaps soon,
very soon,
your destination
strapped in place beside you.

Ecstasy of Motion

You wake with the hotel plumbing.
Kitchen clatter a floor below.
Voices. Doors. Running on stairs.
Laughter like the tearing of cloth.
The tease of a foreign language *containing all secrets.*

You wake with the jet's deep inhalation.
Icke rökare. Non fumeurs. Nicht raucher.
But the plane itself bursts into flame.
Clouds rush inward from all directions.

No matter,—you are in motion.

If you live for a while in Paris, an observer notes,
you don't want to live anywhere, including Paris.
But keep moving.

Warm and drunk with momentum,
lightly tossed in air. Fingerworn
as an old coin.
There is no *loneliness* here, only *solitude.*
No *panic,* but *anticipation.*
No *boredom,* but *idyllic calm.*

Monday flies back into Sunday.
May into April into tiresome March.
You are flying northward, an error of strategy.
You are out-running the sun.
Only the Arctic "wastes" remain.

The same clouds pursue you.
And coil lazily ahead.
Inertia is the basic principle of life, an observer notes,
but inertia means motion. Falling forward. Forever.
But look: we travel to be redeemed by a stranger's handshake,
or a faltering passage of Chopin, in a tenement in East Berlin.
Or a new cloud formation, above the Baltic.

You wake in the genial roar of machinery, flying east.
It might be said you are *in defiance of the sun.*
There are new harsh guttural accents, there are new national
dishes, reindeer freshly shot, blood guaranteed salty
on the tongue. *The secret to travel,* an observer notes,
is very simple: maintain motion.
Don't stop. Don't ask questions.
Don't stop. Don't breathe. Don't despair.
Don't stop.

Boredom

There drifts the sky again.
Here, a single thought crawls slow as a flea.

In one version your yawn is so brutal
the plaster beside your head cracks.
In another version you drown, though not quickly,
in three inches of gray soapy water.

"Last night," says a traveling companion, "I seem to have fallen
asleep with my clothes on. Sitting in a chair by the bed.
All my clothes, my shoes, my wool muffler. Sitting
in a chair by the bed. I woke on the floor but I began
in the chair. When I woke up my first thought was—
Did that creature take my traveler's checks?
My second thought was—*Dear God, are we all still here?*"

When you journey far enough from home, they told us,
the curse will lift.

You wake to the vacuum cleaner's droning overhead,
a menial with hooves, overhead, or is it the odor of disinfectant?—
fingers swollen like white sausage from the bathwater.
Empty freight cars rattle past in your skull,
car after car, rattling, empty, in no hurry.
On schedule.

There drifts the sky again.
Here, a rag is stuffed in your mouth.
Gag. Chew. Swallow. Gag. Smile.
"Your sense of humor is so refreshing!—
did you learn it back in the States?"

In one version your smile is a consequence of the Buddha's blessing.
In another version—"a quick frontal lobotomy performed
with a coat hanger."
And did you really do it yourself? With so little practice?

Here drifts the sky again, through the open window.
The clouds of the North Atlantic, the Baltic, the Dead Sea.
The clouds of the "Free" nations. The captives.
They rise tattered from a traveling companion's cigar.
Foul, and familiar, and comfortable as boredom.
"Is the curse lifting yet," a voice asks,
"or aren't we far enough from home?"

Ecstasy of Boredom at the Berlin Wall

*We must repay both good and evil—
but not necessarily to the person
who did us the good or evil.*
                                    —Nietzsche

In Berlin, at the Wall, it is always high noon.
Which is boring. Which is methodical as history,—clockwork,
and boring. Noon fatigue and concrete and barbed wire
often photographed. Guards and rifles, tourist buses, traffic
moving from west to east. Today is June 17.

East of the Wall?—a charming sepia print.
A fugue of scaffolding and boredom.
The guides speak brightly by rote: statistics, landmarks, monuments.
Trees grow out of bombed churches, which is picturesque
(you may take photographs here) and very boring.
West of the Wall?—the deutsche mark and neon-boredom.
The great Mercedes cross in the night sky.

In Berlin, at the Wall, it is always high noon. Jaws cracking
with ennui. The limit, the end, cement mixers, pansies in pots.
The Wall shreds your fingers, bruises your lips.
The Wall is deafening. The Wall is deaf.
The Wall makes life *serious*, which is always boring.

Overhead, a sun and moon in celestial clockwork.
It is always June 17. Or another day.

        Tourist fatigue of Soviet monuments, gigantic
as the gods' altars. The observer is too dazed to laugh.
Memorials to the slain, or to the victors, so many.
Boredom of Unknown Soldiers, so many.
(I saw a comrade's face split in two by a yawn savage as a hatchet!)

Sudden movements at the Wall are not advised.

        Stupor of "fast-paced" West Berlin, "lively entertainment,"
boredom of neon pornography, Burger King, shoestores grave
as cathedrals. The hardest currency in Europe.

64

On the busy Kantstrasse the martyr Peter Fechter dies again
in propaganda photos amidst the din of tourists.
Flesh billboards overhead, asprawl. Boring the old suicide of Hitler.
Boring the doped-up kids who stagger along the streets, complaining
Life has been serious for so long.

In Berlin, at the Wall, nothing changes.
We have been waiting a very long time.
Fatigue of rifles, chicken wire, tourist buses,
fatigue of passports, crematoria.
At the Wall dying is routine and very boring.

In Berlin, at the Wall, a yawning border guard stoops
to roll a wheeled mirror beneath a car.
But no one is clinging to the axle today.
It is high noon here. A uniformed woman checks passports forever.

It is forever. It is June 17.

Note: June 17 is "German Unity Day"—observed only in the West.

The Great Egg

The Great Egg floats in its perfection
whitely upon the Great Sea of Emptiness

The Great Egg is dazzling smooth and slippery
so beautiful one's heart plunges

This morning there is a crowd of silent people huddled on the Great Egg
we are huddled quite close together on the Great Egg
for the Great Egg is our mother
it will keep us out of the sea
it will keep us from harm

The Great Egg is calcium and protein and white Italian marble
some of us grip its sides with panicked fingers
some with powerful stallions' knees that dare not weaken
some of us lie flat, flat
our burning cheeks against the Egg's calm side

There is no need for prayer on the Great Egg
the Great Egg is prayer floating
upon the Great Sea of Emptiness

In the Great Sea of Emptiness hallucinations routinely arise:
mouths like slashes, children's fingers, angry thrashing animals
seaweed supple as sea-serpents hungry
to loop about one's neck
giant finned creatures with blind blunt horns for eyes
our scientists have not yet defined

When a death occurs on the Great Egg
the body is slipped quietly into the Sea
where wild thrashing and feeding then occur
perhaps someone from the Sea may then climb up
room will be courteously made
the Great Egg is calcium and protein and infinite white marble
the Great Egg can accommodate us all

but it is rare that a death occurs on the Great Egg
death has never been reported on the Great Egg
it is so dazzling smooth and beautiful
floating upon the Great Sea of Emptiness

Children push out of our heads on the Great Egg
and are born without bloodshed or squalling
they take our places when we die
though we rarely die
some of us have never died
as a consequence of the Egg's stony warmth

The Sea of Emptiness is noisy and crowded
with jawbones intestines and razor-fins
there are clumps of jellyfish that are human faces
there are human infants that are in fact imagined
the Sea of Emptiness is itself imagined
our philosophers doubt its existence
our theoreticians see nothing there
the Sea is impatient with appetite which is an illusion
the Sea is noisy which is grammar without language
the Sea is untidy lapping about the sides of the Great Egg

The Great Egg dropped from the sky many centuries ago
laid by an enormous golden eagle whose wings darkened the sun
or was it a fragment of moon rock
or a sacred tear of God's that, in falling, froze to stone—?
Our historians are in conflict, our linguists and poets busy
themselves in conflict, the origin of the Great Egg is a mystery
but no matter: it is beautiful this morning
in its creamy-pale symmetry
in its calcium warmth
floating upon the Great Sea of Emptiness
where nothing organic resides
where the tissue of grammar does not exist

our astronomers have measured nothing there
our philosophers and soldiers have measured nothing there
the Great Egg floats in its perfection
it is so dazzling smooth
it is so beautiful
one's heart plunges

The Child-Bride

Fortunately for you I am resurrected in one piece, or nearly.
In my ancient wedding gown. With my mummy's wise grimace.
My skull partly covered with hairy moss, the lace at my wrists
grown into my wrists, my eye-sockets not quite eyeless.
Much publicity, of course, attends my resurrection.

Approximately four-feet-four-inches tall, in life.
Approximately eleven years of age.

I am resurrected gently, with caution. With gauze, tweezers,
patience. *The bridal gown used as a shroud, an old custom.*
Buried with her own infant.

I am immortal, my hide is weathered and thick,
I am brittle, I may fall apart, here is my wedding ring,
here is my gold cross, my bracelet of braided hair.
I am sorry if I have frightened you.

Resurrected from my grave after centuries of sleep,
resurrected in one remarkable piece. Or nearly.
Overhead the raw North Atlantic sky, on all sides
nibbled grave-mounds and eroded crosses and winds funnelled
to a howl, centuries, days, each day the same day,
each hour weathering my shy smile into this grimace.
Everywhere in the soil bones, bone-fragments, bone-dust.
The bones of human beings, the bones of rats, mice, sheep.

The same dwarf sheep wander the island, clumsy, grazing
calm and sure-footed amid the rocks, the broken crosses,
the moss. Starving, rheumy-eyed, unhurried, the same sheep,
approximately eleven years of age, a child-bride, buried
with her own infant, her skin mummified though not "perfectly
preserved"—

Fortunately for you I offer no resistance, I am a curiosity
under no spell of evil, I bring no curse, my husband lies
nearby but I have forgotten him, my mother, all my mothers,

69

my sisters, brothers, perhaps I had husbands, bone
and bone-fragments and bone-dust, relics, crosses grown
into the skeleton, the tiny bones of mice and birds ground
into the soil, we might all be resurrected with tweezers.
What do the dead know, what is their secret—

Much publicity, of course, attends my resurrection.
But it has all happened long ago.
But it is the same hour.
The bridal gown used as a shroud, an old custom.

High-Wire Artist

Down there?
It is not God, it is only the sawdust floor.

Tonight I am spangled with light, I burn your staring eyes.
Unlike you on the ground I am shadowless
for the high wire admits no shadows.

Watch me move like a sleepwalker!
—the eight-foot bar horizontal at my sequined chest, my bare
blind feet shrewdly groping—
my right foot, and then my left, and then my right—

It must be a parable, you say. An allegory.
It must be more than a mere tightrope walker.
For why does the crowd stare so intently,
why is the arena hushed?

There are, of course, days of travel on the surface of the earth.
Days of dark chill rains.
Days of over-eating and hotel stupor and newsprint and alcohol.
Days of getting through days.
Nights of getting through nights.
Sometimes I forget: am I dead now, or still alive.
Have I fallen yet, have the headlines made their proclamation?—
or am I still alive.

Watch: four or five quick steps and then a pause
as the wire vibrates in the wind.
It isn't generally known, how the wire vibrates in the wind.
There *is* danger, your tickets *are* worth the price,
but I don't intend to fall tonight.
See how gracefully I regain my balance,
how, though I am in a panicked crouch,
my knees do not tremble.
As you stare in silence, waiting.

Life on the ground with the rest of you?—the flat-footed ground?
Life in a visible body, in ordinary flesh and bone?

As I have said in previous interviews, it is tolerable
if seen as an interruption of the high-wire act.
And the high-wire act is tolerable in terms of its reward:
a safe descent to earth.

Pray? On the high wire?
Why?
On the high wire prayer does no good.
And on the ground, of course, there is no need.
On the ground there is certainly no need.

After all it is not God that beckons, only the sawdust,
that shallow abyss.
Which I know very well and will risk for you,
for the price of your tickets.

Homage to Virginia Woolf

I walked into the river and the river greedily arose.
It must have been waiting for years. It must have felt no alarm.

The finest hour of my life?—the final page, the punctuation,
the relief of escaping madness.
The solace of never being required to *begin again.*

I walked into the river and bells rang in a drunken frenzy.
It must have been a wedding, for strangers pressed their wet mouths
    against mine.
Giant fish nibbled at my toes like lovers.

An invisible woman sinking, staggering, being carried down-
    stream, heavier than one would have thought.
And far more stubborn.

A fin passing far out—look, how it turns, how it curves near!

This is the finest hour of my life, this completion.
Waves upon waves, no end to them, but no thought, no brain
    to think, no fevered beating, no voice.

(I like, I once gaily said, to go out of the room talking,
an unfinished casual sentence on my lips.)

I walked into the river and the river greedily arose.
Left behind was the racket of life!—the whirring terror of death!
The eclipse deepening around Roger's grave!
And is this War not the doom of our civilization?
I think it is. I think it must be. I do not care to survive.

But in my diary, as you all shall see, I noted *Haddock and sausage meat:*
One gains a certain hold on sausage and haddock
by writing them down.

One gains a certain hold on one's life
by boldly casting it aside.

A Report to an Academy

(after Kafka)

No way out.
A three-sided cage nailed to a locker:
the ceiling against the nape of my neck,
the narrow sides cutting into my thighs.

Impossible to stand. Or to sit.
Impossible to sleep.
My captors had constructed the perfect cage:
impossible to forget.
So I squatted in the corner, my knees trembling.

No way out.
A statement that, perhaps, you cannot comprehend.
No way out.

Squatting in the cage.
Sobbing. No way out.
Picking at fleas. Sobbing.
Over and over the knowledge:
I must find a way out or die.

Freedom?
But no. Please do not misunderstand.
Esteemed ladies and gentlemen, please do not misunderstand.
Freedom was never a choice: only a way out.

Though it is difficult for you, ladies and gentlemen,
you must try to imagine a three-sided cage:
the ceiling against the nape of my neck,
the narrow sides cutting into my thighs,
the bars raising welts on my hide.

Bound for the zoological garden where on Sundays
you and your children would dawdle, grinning
and pointing, whistling, *Isn't he ugly, isn't he funny,*
tossing peanuts into my cage, or crusts of bread,
or sharp stones.

Bound for the zoological garden and a more spacious cage
I saw that freedom was not a choice.
Freedom is not a word in an ape's vocabulary.

Consequently I became one of you.

I charmed my captors, I learned their speech,
I grew wonderfully cunning, I now wear a necktie.

Please do not misunderstand, esteemed ladies and gentlemen:
I am not bitter.
I had to find a way out of the cage or die.
So I became one of you. As you see.

The first thing I learned from my captors was a frank handshake,
which I practice every day.
Will you give me your hand?

V.

Selected Poems
1970–1978

Abandoned Airfield, 1977

for my father, Frederick Oates

In grass the cinder runways are hidden:
in grasses taller than children.
Nothing springs into movement but there is motion
    on all sides—
the shadows of low-flying planes
thinning to the shadows of starlings—
the trembling of pollen, the iridescence of black flies.
Above the corrugated roof a wind-sock flutters
    in gray shreds.
Thirty years. Thirty-five years.

Today's winds come from all directions.

Though it is Sunday there are no Piper Cubs circling
    to land,
there are no cars parked in the lot,
there are no children screaming with excitement
as their fathers test the sky.
The day's flying is over. It is nearly dusk.
The lightweight planes have dipped and soared and plunged
and fallen and righted themselves and risen and skimmed
low over that line of willows by the creek:
they have prepared soberly to land to taxi along the runway
to slow to come to rest to lie in broken rusted hulks.
The airfield is empty. The pilots sleep.
Exhausted, they feel the winds blow over them,
the grasses waving languidly above their heads.

Strange children have broken into the hangar,
have wrenched a door off its hinges.
Strange to us, the smears of tar and the smashed glass
and the small droning winds.
Who are we to survive those clumsy flights?
To recall the jarring thud of the plane's wheels
and the rightness of the cindery earth
and the sunburnt alarm of children who must witness
their fathers riding the air,

garish and frail as kites?

Now the field belongs to starlings.
Irritated by our presence they rise squawking
where gravity tosses them
and we cannot follow.

Dreaming America

for my mother, Carolina Oates

When the two-lane highway was widened
the animals retreated.
Skunks, raccoons, rabbits,—even their small corpses
were transformed into rags
and then into designs
and then into stains
then nothing.

When the highway was linked to another
and to another
six lanes, then nine, then twelve arose
sweeping nobly to the horizon
along measured white lines.
The polled Herefords were sold.
The barbed-wire fences dismantled.
When the cornfields were bulldozed
the farmhouses turned to shanties;
the barns fell;
the silos collapsed.

When the fields were paved over
Frisch's Big Boy reared seventy feet in the air.
Sunoco and *Texaco* and *Gulf* signs gaily competed
on hundred-foot stilts.
Eyeballs on stalks:
miraculous!
And illuminated all night.

Where that useless stretch of poplars lay
an orange sphere of gigantic proportions
announces *Wonderland East*, open
for Thursday evening shopping.
Here, tonight, packs of teenagers hunt
one another.
The terrazzo footprints are known by heart.

Where did the country go?—cry the travelers, soaring

past. *Where did the country go?*—ask the strangers.
The teenagers never ask.

Where sway-backed horses once grazed in a dream that had no history,
tonight a thirteen-year-old girl stands dreaming
into the window of Levitz's Records & Hi-Fi Equipment.
We drive past, our speed accelerating. We disappear.
We return.

Last Harvest

That last harvest the cornfields were paved
the newts were translated to jets' keening wails
everywhere I stumbled I turned to look back
everywhere creatures froze cunning as stone

A sweep of my massive hand crushed a city
winds rushed together like a knot
when I snorted with laughter
innocent as a gale

That last harvest the bubble of a globe
floated weightless into the night
yawning I felt something tug at my eyelids
I felt gravity itself turning to ice

I sickened and lay across continents
my fingers scooped waves of sand
my great head went hollow with grief
losing one by one the sacred words
harvest, gale, bubble, globe, grief

Visionary Adventures of a Wild Dog Pack

Snow-stubbled January fields and evil
frozen between our toes
by the time you see us
it is already too late
we trot across the vegetable world
in a pack of mad teeth and tongues

Voices in you speak
to our furious sorrow
we hear nothing
we are mute
we are worm-ridden
bullet-shy
starving-crafty
we lap at pools of Arctic cold and give thanks
we devour garbage
teeth and tongues and rib-rippling sides
giving perpetual thanks

Look: a pack of stomachs
covered in snarled fur!

Once over-loved we are now displaced
last summer's pets abandoned
by the roadside
not even lonely now
forgetful of our old names
grunting and whining and whimpering with cold
a pack of stomachs roused at dusk
tongues aslant in stained mouths

We look like laughter, don't we?
tearing these feathery things apart
flinging the blood into the air
we charge in a pack
we whine and dodge and flee
savage-sad
wise mouths and guts

giving perpetual thanks

Voices in you speak
to our mute sorrow
we hear nothing
a pack of stomachs covered in snarled fur
roused starving at dusk

Fertilizing the Continent

Fluid as music we pass through,
and return, bringing ancestors
to this new place:
our childhood bones merging, melting.
The map's old divisions snarl, breaking
as we pass invisibly through.

The continent takes us on,
and begins now to dream us:
worlds shading into worlds.
What integrity in our bones' fated structure?—
a new language dispels it.
A new meridian, a new alchemy
of sun and spangled shade.

Rituals seek to enter us,
—as if the body were a sacred event.

After Terror. . . .

       . . . We move like the slow
reverent fingers of the blind.
Our negotiating of what remains of us
is a prayer cleverly worked out
in flesh.

We pray to what has not yet happened.

Cautious, we look up. The move is bold.
We decipher the code that now surrounds us.
It is all protein, all oxygen, all new,
and must be learned.

It is interior as the roofs of our mouths.

"Promiscuity"

> *Erthe upon erthe is wonderly wrought*
> *Erthe upon erthe hath worship of nought. . . .*
> —medieval poem

* No choice.

* A slow circling parade. Shuffling
  of anonymous feet.
  Imperfect destinies to mock
  a "perfect destiny."

* Each time the camera advanced
  smiles leapt forward.
  So eager.

* On Fridays, Discount Foods open until 9.
  The decks of a sickened ship,
  aisles awash with shapes—
  crates half-unpacked,
  pyramids of cans,
  women pushing shopping carts
  balky as wire animals.
  Children run free, freely
  in the aisles.

* Studying the jet's contrails
  I think of you, always
  of you: but have forgotten why.

* It declared itself a mountain,
  it had storybook icy peaks.
  But by June it had begun to thaw.
  By August, even the rivulets at the base
  had dried.
  No one has drowned.
  No one misses the drama
  of the storybook peaks.

The Suicide

didn't acknowledge receipt
didn't wave goodbye
didn't flutter the air with kisses
a mound of tinsel gifts unwrapped
air mail letters unopened
bedclothes rumpled
No thank you

always elsewhere

though it was raining elsewhere
though strange-speaking persons peopled the streets
the minarets might have been dangerous
the drinking water suspect
though we at home slaved and baked
and wept and dialled the phone
and hung tinsel ornaments
did he marvel
did he thank

was he grateful   did he know
was he considerate
was he human .
was he there

Always elsewhere!
didn't thank
didn't kiss
toothbrush stiffened
cat scratching at the screen
car battery dead

was that human?

Went where?

Firing a Field

in memory of Flannery O'Connor

Unbelievers, look! there the taut darts of flame
unravel the landscape
the farmer and his sons salute the blaze
as if it were something of day
and not night

Who can follow us into such meanness?

Not night
not the fleeing furry creatures
the grouse's wings wildly beating
the crackle of thistles
the applause of flames

Beating at the underside of the head

After this magisterial burning
the rabbits won't dare to enter our gardens
the porcupines will whine in exile
    licking their scorched feet
the insects' drone will be silenced
the slovenly moths and their wings of white-beaten gold
mute with defeat
mute with defeat
all the unbelievers
by their own mannerly instincts repelled

Who can follow us into such meanness?

After this final burning
and the field stubbled with black
punished for so much sunlight
and the cartwheels of butterflies loving
    in stark daylight
orioles scattered back to the trees
the love songs of ants roasted crisp
wasps popping like tiny grenades

and small soft animals beaten limp as rags
watersoaked in panic

Let all creatures lie loosely dead:
for were we not granted dominion over them?

After this fire that darts from our fingers
the groundhogs' burrows filled in at last, mere graves
toadstools crushed soft beneath Christ's bare feet
our revenge sifts downward like falling ash
falling kingly
upon what was Creation

Shelley at Viareggio

Child-shapes in the waves beckoned. I saw.
Hands churning lewdly into foam.
The faces turned crystal, the voices rang:
"Don't abandon us, come
to us,
you are of us,
we are your children."

Here I am dancing barefoot through the surf,
leaping weightless in the mist.
My heartbeat pounds away harsh things.
My syllables overcome the waves.
Nothing slows me, I squirm snakily free,
whose fingers are those, closing about my wrist—?
O I loathe you!—and you!—inside my boy's smile.
O I grant enchantment!

I think those are fig trees, coarse tricky shapes.
I have no use for them, they cannot dance.
I cry to the sea: "Will you take this slave
of Music, this slave, slavish to thee, enslaved
to Thee, the swimming dream of Thee
I have invented . . . ?"

Look, the water dense and mottled with foam,
grizzled as peasants' beards!

The faces I loved were one face.
They turned to haze beneath my music.
My smile transformed the ugliest of faces,
—my miracle therefore!
(How I loathed the boat that fought
to keep its crude life,
the topsails thundering in protest.)

But my schoolboy jacket was weighted:
Lamia on one side, Aeschylus on the other.
Flesh struggled ignobly to swim.
Even the sea birds shrieked.
The children drew me down, with their mirror.
My dearest Self, on the sea-bed, calmed.
Sweet-rotting iridescent teeth,
eyes sightless and pure,
purer than those famous pearls!
O stubborn in purity in loathing!

I go on, I once said, till I am stopped.
But I never am stopped.
Save by the ugly heaped rocks
at Viareggio.

Domestic Miracles

*   a stampede of hooves
     must have bruised my thighs
     to such iridescent blooms

*   a sweet rot rises
     from the pages long dried:
     the diary now so warped
     my hand cannot caress it

*   strangers' children swim
     in those oil-slick waves
     their shouts and arms white
     their joy like drowning:
     yet joy

*   My love: you make me permanent
     like old unlovely clay relics
     unearthed in the Egypt
     of the ancient dead

In your presence the soul between us speaks:
Something miraculous has happened.

How Gentle

how gentle are we rising
easy as eyes in sockets turning

intimate the hardness: jaw
upon jaw, forehead warm

upon forehead
kisses quick as breaths, without volition

Love: I am luminous
careless as love's breathing

fluorescent glowing the fine
warm veins and bones

your weight,
the sky lowered suddenly

I am loved: a message
clanging of a bell in silence

you are quickened with surprise
our horizons surrender to walls

Are we wearing out
our skins' defenses?—

turning to silk, texture of flashy
airy surfaces scant as breaths?

I am loved: the noon slides gently
suddenly upon us
to wake us

Skyscape

The entire morning drew my gaze
I saw no shape I knew
not clouds but human figures
a battalion of statues darkening the sky

These were presences to weigh harshly
against the unprotected eye
but there was no harm to them
no terror in their infinite calm

I saw no shape I knew

I saw everyone:
men who were granite columns
women in an ecstasy of white marble,
children dwarfed by seraphim's wings

Stately and regal as clouds
transformed white and smoothly perfect
all those stony brows
those egg-like sightless eyes

Their muscled flesh is prodigious
and uncontaminated by the heat of our blood
warriors, gargoyles, horses, women
who have borne stone children out of their stony loins

Oblivious of our worship and our dread
they pass in their methodical calm
transformed ruthless in beauty
massive, perfect, moon-pale, merely rock

Ice Age

The Spirit moves where it will:
the air is scimitars, the air is platinum.

All night we have heard the living flesh of trees crack.
We have heard the pain, the awful silence.
And in the morning the ear is deafened in white.

A world of glass!—many-winged glare of glass.
If the pulse beats in this Ice Age it must learn caution,
for here the slightest touch kills.

Razor cruel, that light from the east.
We walk in blinded circles, helpless.
Willows—poplars—evergreens—a Russian olive:
the ice-drowse is upon us, the hypnosis
of ancient sleep.

In the Ice Age beauty fits tight as a mask of skin.
One cannot breathe, one stiffens to perfection.
There are no outcries.

Afterword

A volume of "selected poems" forces a sense of both responsibility and mortality upon the poet. The pleasure of selection—of choosing, discriminating, judging, weeding out—soon becomes an unanticipated ordeal. One is pulled in contradictory directions: there is the wish to preserve the past, which is, after all, a kind of miniature history of the self; there is the natural wish to remake the past—perhaps even to remake history. In assembling poems for this volume I have chosen only those from earlier collections that can be gracefully assimilated into the structure suggested by the newer work—that is, those relevant to the thematic concerns of "Invisible Woman"; and those that struck me as recognizable, in however diffracted and oblique a way, as my own. If I have omitted a fair number of earlier poems, including my entire first book, it isn't so much that I have rejected them as poems, as that I fail to recognize my own voice in them. I feel no kinship, no sense of continuity. That aspect of the past is finally *past*—and cannot be retrieved.

The theme of invisibility has haunted me for many years, since earliest girlhood. A woman often feels "invisible" in a public sense precisely because her physical being—her "visibility"—figures so prominently in her identity. She is judged as a body, she is "attractive" or "unattractive," while knowing that her deepest self is inward, and secret: knowing, *hoping* that her spiritual essence is a great deal more complex than the casual eye of the observer will allow. It might be argued that the poet, inhabiting a consciousness and a voice, is "invisible" as well; it might be argued that all persons, defined to themselves rather more as what they think and dream, than what they do, are "invisible." Hence, the preoccupation of the majority of these poems.

Joyce Carol Oates

ONTARIO REVIEW PRESS POETRY SERIES